Manifesto
for the
Abolition of
Enslavement to Interest on Money

with explanations provided
by
Gottfried Feder, Dipl.Engineer

1 9 1 9

Originally Published by Joseph C. Hubers Verlag,
Diessen vor Muenchen, Germany

Translated into English by Hadding Scott, 2012
ISBN: 978-1537435336 2016

Black Kite Publishing
ISBN: 978-0-9957215-3-1 2017

Contents

The Manifesto for the Abolition of Enslavement to Interest on Money
   a. What is Mammonism?
   b. What is the cure for Mammonism?
   c. The nine points of the Manifesto.

Implementation and Rationale
1. Because of failed promises of the German Revolution of 1918 the people are tending more and more toward Bolshevism.
2. The German folk are sick with Mammonism.
3. Mammonism derives its power from interest on loans.
4. The way to cure Mammonism is by abolishing interest on loans, especially war-bonds.
5. The vast majority of Germans holding war-bonds really lose money because of them, because they have to pay taxes to cover the interest payments; only the largest holders of war-bonds have a net profit from them.
6. Germany's real wealth consists not in any material assets but in the productivity of the German people.
7. If the obligation to pay interest on public debt were ended, the Bavarian state could abolish all direct and indirect taxes and fund itself entirely on the revenues from state-owned industries.
8. Interest-payments are the reason why the state cannot do without taxes; those receiving the largest

sums of interest pay relatively little in taxes. The Reich is financially in a much worse situations than the federal state.
9. Comparison of the affluent bondholder, the working-class bondholder, and the dependent bondholder. Expansion of social welfare for the dependent bondholder after cancellation of interest.
10. Instead of repaying the principal of war-bonds under cancellation of interest the state could simply declared the bonds to be currency.
11. For other fixed-interest assets, including mortgages, repayment under cancellation of interest is recommended. This should solve the housing problem.
12. A history of opposition to interest -slavery.
    a. Curtailment and prohibition of interest before the 19th century.
    b. Enshrinement of interest under the developing global order during the 19th century.
c. Cancellation of interest will dissolve the interest-community within Germany and enables the German nation to unite against the Gold International.

The Conversion of War-Bonds into Bank-Credit

Rather than simply declare war-bonds to be currency, a better idea is to require that they be surrendered for conversion into bank-credit.

Special Comments on the Demand for Laws in the

Manifesto
Elaboration of the nine points.

The Objections and their Refutation
Objections from various perspectives are addressed.
    a. Three objections based on a failure to comprehend how conditions would change under abolition of interest-slavery.
- b. A question from the perspective of a large bondholder.
- c. How is depriving investors of interest supposed to help the worker?
- d. What about the importance of inheritance in holding families together?
- e. Three objections from officials of the current system.
- f. The Communist complaint that abolition of interest will not abolish economic inequality.
    g. Social-Democracy is doomed because it is based on Marxist ideology, which does not recognize the radical difference between industrial capital and loan-capital. Social-Democratic government, as a moderate application of Marxism that fails, paves the way for Communism.
    h. The contemptible bourgeois and two objections from the bourgeois perspective. *Won't abolition of interest adversely affect savings?* No. *Is big loan-capital really not in some way productive?* Only labor is productive.

Further Program
   a. Abolition of interest-slavery is the prerequisite for establishment of the social state.
   b. Reconstruction of the German

state according to the true spirit of socialism.
   c. Liberation of the entire world from Jewish control.

Manifesto for the Abolition of Enslavement to Interest on Money

Mammonism is the heavy, all- encompassing and overwhelming sickness from which our contemporary cultural sphere, and indeed all mankind, suffers. It is like a devastating illness, like a devouring poison that has gripped the peoples of the world.

By Mammonism is to be understood:

on the one hand, the overwhelming international money-powers, the supragovernmental financial power enthroned above any right of self-determination of peoples, international big capital, the purely Gold International;

on the other hand, a mindset that has taken hold of the broadest circle of peoples; the insatiable lust for gain, the purely worldly-oriented conception of life that has already led to a frightening decline of all moral concepts and can only lead to more.

This mindset is embodied and reaches its acme in international plutocracy.

The chief source of power for Mammonism is the effortless and endless income that is produced through interest.

From the thoroughly immoral idea of interest on loans the Gold International was born. The mental and moral constitution grown from the lust for interest and profiteering of every kind has led to the frightening corruption of a part of the bourgeoisie.

The idea of interest on loans is the diabolical invention of big loan-capital; it alone makes possible the lazy drone's life of a minority of tycoons at the expense of the productive peoples and their work-potential; it has led to profound, irreconcilable differences, to class-hatred, from which war among citizens and brothers was born.

The only cure, the radical means to heal suffering humanity is

the abolition of enslavement to interest on money.

The abolition of enslavement to interest on money signifies the only possible and conclusive liberation of productive labor from the hidden coercive money- powers.

The abolition of enslavement to interest signifies the restoration of the free personality, the redemption of man from slavery, from the curse whereby Mammonism has bound his soul.
Whoever wishes to fight capitalism, must abolish enslavement to interest.

Where must the abolition of enslavement to interest

begin? *With loan-capital!*

Why?

Because loan-capital, compared to all industrial big capital, is so overpowering that the great money-powers can only be fought effectively through the abolition of interest-slavery. 20:1 is the proportion of loan-capital to industrial big capital. The German people must annually raise more than 12 billion in interest for loan-capital in the form of direct and indirect taxes, rent, and the rising cost of living, while even in the boom-years of the war the sum-total of all dividends distributed by the German joint-stock companies amounted to only 1 billion.

The *avalanche-like growth* of loan-capital surpasses all human capacity for calculation, through eternal, endless, and effortless income from interest, and from interest on interest.

What blessing does the abolition of enslavement to interest bring for the laboring folk of Germany, for the proletarians of all countries of the Earth?

The abolition of enslavement to interest gives us the possibility of pursuing *the repeal of all direct and indirect taxes*. Hear this, you value-producing men of all lands, all states and continents: all state revenues flowing from direct and indirect sources pour constantly into the pockets of big loan-capital.

The profits of state-owned businesses, including the

postal service, telegraph, telephone, railroad, mines, forests, and so on, suffice entirely for the funding of all essential state commitments for schools, universities, courts, administrative agencies, and social welfare.

Thus no true socialism will bring any blessing to humanity as long as the profits from public enterprises remain tributary to big loan-capital.

Therefore we demand as a fundamental law of the state, first for the German peoples, then as a fundamental law for all those kindred peoples that wish to enter with us into the cultural community of a league of nations, the following:

> § 1. War-bonds, along with all other debt-instruments of the German Reich, along with all other debt-instruments of the German federal states, especially railroad-bonds, as well as debenture-bonds of all local governments, are declared, under cancellation of the obligation for interest, to be legal tender for the face-value [or rather are to be converted into bank-credit].

§ 2. With all other fixed-interest papers, covered bonds, industrial bonds, mortgages, *etc.*, the obligation for interest is replaced by the obligation to repay the principal; thus after 20 or 25 years, depending on the interest- rate, the lent capital is repaid and the debt retired.

§ 3. All real-estate debts, mortgages, *etc.*, are to be paid off on installments of the same amount as the payments required hitherto, in keeping with the charges recorded in the land-register. The property in houses and land freed from debt in this manner becomes partly the property of the state or of the local government. [In this way the state becomes better situated to control and to lower rents.]

§ 4. The entire monetary system should be under the state's central bank. All private banks likewise; postal-check banks, savings banks, and credit unions, all become affiliated as branch-operations.

§ 5. All credit for real estate is awarded only through the state's bank. Personal credit and commercial credit are mandated to private bankers under a concession from the state. This concession is granted based on consideration of need, with a ban on the establishment of branches for certain districts. The scale of charges is fixed by the state.

§ 6. Equity-securities are paid off in the same manner as fixed- interest papers at the annual rate of 5%. Excess profits are paid out in part to the stockholders as compensation for "risked" capital (in contrast to fixed-interest and coin-backed papers), while the remaining surplus, by the sovereign right of labor, is either socially distributed or applied for the reduction of the prices of products.

§ 7. For all persons who for physical reasons

(advanced age, illness, physical or mental work-disability, extreme youth) are not in a position to earn their livelihood, the interest-incomes from present capital assets continue to be paid as a pension at the same, and eventually even increased levels, in return for delivery of securities.

§ 8. In the interest of a reduction of the current inflation of paper money, a universal, strongly graduated tax on war-bond certificates and other debt- instruments of the Reich and of states is enacted. These papers are to be pulped.

§ 9. Through intensive enlightenment of the people, it is to be made clear to the people that money is and should be nothing other than a voucher for completed labor; that while every highly developed economy of course has need of money as a medium of exchange, the function of money also ends with that, and in no case should money be lent a supramundane power to grow of itself by means of interest, at the expense of productive labor.

Why have we not already done all this, which is so self-evident, which must be regarded as the Egg of Columbus for the social question?

Because in our Mammonistic blindness we have unlearned how to see clearly that the doctrine of the sanctity of interest is a monstrous self-deception, that the gospel of the loan-interest that alone makes one blessed has entangled our entire thinking in the golden web of international plutocracy. Because we have forgotten and are deliberately kept in confusion by the omnipotent money-powers about the fact that -- except in the case of a few rich people -- the interest that seems so lovely, and is so beloved of the thoughtless, is completely offset by taxes. All of our tax-legislation is and remains, so long as we do not have liberation from enslavement to interest, only a tribute-obligation to big capital, and not, as we would imagine, a voluntary sacrifice for the accomplishment of labor for the community.

Therefore liberation from enslavement to interest on money is the clear motto for the global revolution, for the liberation of productive labor from the chains of the supragovernmental money-powers.

Implementation and Rationale

We stand in the midst of one of the most grievous crises that our impoverished folk has had to endure in its painful history. Seriously ill is our folk; seriously ill is the entire world.
Helplessly the nations stammer; a passionate longing, a cry for redemption passes through the gloomy masses. With laughter and dancing, with cinema and pageantry, the folk seeks to forget its own lamentable destiny -- to forget about its disillusioned hopes, about the deep inner pain, about the terrible disappointment over what one would so gladly call "gains of the revolution." But how did we imagine it all differently?

How did all the fine promises run differently?

All that we hoped to gain in the dark of night, in the darkness of our military collapse, seemed to be glistening gold, but now, when the gray day illuminates the find, it is all rotten bits of wood. Now we stand here at a loss. For the sake of these rotten bits of wood that shone so finely in the night, we have thrown away everything that hitherto was dear and valuable to us, and have stuffed all our pockets with this lamentable trove. No wonder that the rage of despair grips precisely the poorest of the poor, and that they rage in senseless wrath against their own brothers, and in their deep longing for redemption seek to destroy all that stands in the way. This condition must lead to utter madness, if consciencelessness and stupidity goad the people further.

And whither this madness leads, we see in Bolshevik Russia. Nationalization, as socialization is called in Russia, has proven to be a failure, declares an unperturbed Lenin. The economy is destroyed, the buying-power of money down to nothing, the intelligentsia killed, the laborer without bread. Despair in the entire people; only bloody terror based on Chinese and Latvian mercenaries is able to protect the Red dictators from the vengeance of the betrayed folk. Among us too the development will follow this course, if international speculators, obsessed party-fanatics, representatives of the most grievously burdened bourgeoisie, and members of a race most deeply alien in nature to the German folk, continue to be allowed in the government. What indeed were those pretty, pretty words that one whispered into our ear?

Negotiated peace, League of Nations, parliamentarism, sovereignty of the people, democracy, dictatorship of the proletariat, socialism, destruction of capitalism, liberation from militarism, and other such pretty slogans. A new free people was supposed to arise, which should determine its own destiny.

None of any of that has come true, was able to come true, or ever could come true, if we do not with the highest moral seriousness investigate all these apparitions, all these slogans -- if we do not conscientiously test the symptoms of the illness like an intelligent, concerned physician, and painstakingly diagnose the present condition of the sick person, sparing no effort to ascertain whence this serious critical illness arises.

* * * * *

The sickness of our age is called Mammonism.

What is Mammonism?
Mammonism is the sinister, invisible, mysterious reign of the great international money-powers.
Mammonism is however also a mindset; it is the worship of these money-powers on the part of all those who are infected with the Mammonistic poison.
Mammonism is the unlimited hypertrophy of the -- in itself healthy -- human drive for acquisition.
Mammonism is the lust for money grown into a madness, which knows no higher goal than to pile money on top of money, which seeks with unequaled

brutality to coerce all forces of the world into its service, and must lead to the economic enslavement, to the exploitation of the work-potential of all peoples of the world. Mammonism is the mindset that has led to a decline of all moral concepts. Mammonism considered as a worldwide phenomenon is to be equated with brutal, ruthless egoism in man.

Mammonism is the spirit of greed, of boundless desire to rule, of the mentality entirely focused on seizing the goods and treasures of the world; it is at its core the religion of the purely worldly- oriented human type.

Mammonism is the direct opposite of socialism. Socialism, conceived as the highest moral idea, as the idea that man is not in the world only for himself alone, that every man has duties toward
the community, toward all humanity, and that he is not only responsible for the momentary wellbeing of his family, of the members of his tribe, of his folk, but that he also has unshakable moral obligations toward the future of his children and his folk.

More concretely, we must see Mammonism as the conscious collusion of the power-hungry big capitalists of all peoples. Noteworthy in this has always been the hidden arrival of Mammonism.

The big tycoons lurk indeed as the ultimate driving force behind world- encompassing Anglo-American imperialism; nothing else. The great money-powers indeed financed the terrifying mass-homicides of the World War. The great money-powers have indeed, as owners of all great newspapers, woven the world into a web of lies. They have with satisfaction whipped up all lower passions, have diligently fostered the growth of present tendencies, and have through clever press-propaganda brought French revanchism to a boil. They carefully nurtured the Pan-Slavic idea, the Serbian conceit of being a great power, and the need of these states for money, to the point that the world conflagration must ignite.

Even among us in Germany the spirit of Mammonism that wanted to know only more export-figures, national wealth, expansion, big bank projects, and international finance deals, led to a rout of public morality, to the decline of our ruling circle into materialism and hedonism, to a superficiality in our national life, all factors that share blame for the terrifying collapse.

* * * * *

With astonishment we must ask ourselves whence Mammonism, whence international big capital derives its irresistible power.

It is not to be overlooked that the international collaboration of the great money-powers represents a completely new phenomenon. We have no parallel for this in history. International obligations of a monetary nature were practically unknown. Only with the rising global economy, with general global commerce, did the idea of international interest-economy establish itself, and here we touch the deepest root, here we have hit upon the innermost source of strength from which the Golden International draws its irresistible power.

Interest, the effortless and endless influx of goods based on the mere ownership of money without any addition of labor, has caused the great money-powers to grow. Loan-interest is the diabolical principle from which the Gold International was born. Loan- capital has firmly attached its blood- funnel absolutely everywhere. Like the arms of an anemone big loan capital has ensnared all states, all peoples of the world.

Government loans, government bonds, railroad bonds, war bonds, mortgages, covered-bond obligations -- in short loan-instruments of every kind have in a manner ensnared our entire economic life, so that henceforth all the peoples of the world wriggle helplessly in the golden webs. For the sake of the interest-principle, in keeping with a thoroughly mad political delusion that every kind of possession carries an entitlement to earnings, we have submitted to *enslavement to interest on money*. Not a single real, valid moral reason can be given as to why mere possession of money should bring an entitlement to perpetual interest- payments.

This inner opposition to interest, and to income of every kind without any occurrence of productive labor, extends through the soul-life of all peoples and times. But never has this deep inner resistance to the power of money become so conscious for the nations as in our time.

Never has Mammonism been prepared in such a world-encompassing manner to begin world-domination. Never yet has it placed in its service all baseness, lust for power, lust for revenge, greed, envy, and falsehood in such a cleverly concealed and yet brutally pushy manner as now. The World War is at its inmost core one of the biggest decisions in the evolutionary process of humanity in the struggle to decide whether in the future the Mammonistic-materialistic worldview or the socialistic-aristocratic worldview should determine the fate of the world.

* * * * *

On the surface, the Mammonistic Anglo-American coalition has without a doubt been initially victorious. As a reaction against it, Bolshevism arose in the East, and if one wishes to see a great idea in Bolshevism, it is without a doubt the position diametrically opposed to the Mammonistic worldview. The methods that Bolshevism seeks to employ for this however are the botched cures of a Dr. Eisenbarth. They are the attempt to help someone sick from internal poisoning with a scalpel, by amputating his head, arm, and legs.

Against this rampage of Bolshevism, against this senseless overturning, we must present a workable new idea that with unifying force unites all laboring classes, so as to drive out the poison that has made the world sick.

I see this means in the abolition of enslavement to interest on money.

There are three factors that make interest on loan-capital conspicuous as the authentic and true cause of our financial misery.

First, the monstrous disproportion of fixed-interest loan-capital, thus of capital that grows of its own accord without application of creative labor, and indeed grows on forever. Among us in Germany this loan-capital has already reached a level that we do not consider too high at 250 billion. In contrast to this enormous sum, the industrial working capital of our entire German industry stands at only 11.8 billion. In addition there is the 3.5 billion in capital of the 16,000 industrial limited-liability companies [G.m.b.H], so that altogether we have only about 15 billion in industrial capital to tabulate. *20:1 is the first fundamental finding.* [* Obviously 17:1 is more accurate, but maybe Feder is allowing for the likelihood that the proportion will increase.]

This appraisal means that in financial problems of the largest importance, all measures concerned with loan-capital must prove 20 times as effective as measures directed at industrial big capital.

Second: the interest-payment on the loan-capital above, estimated at 250 billion, considered in its totality for all times, amounts to about 12½ billion annually. By contrast, the sum-total of all industrial dividends distributed in the year 1916 amounted in the year 1915 to about one billion marks. In the preceding decades this number was, on the average, about 600 million. In the last two years of the war [1914-1918] it may very well have gone up considerably, but will record an all-the- greater crash for the current year [1919].

The average profitability of all German stock-corporations [*A.G.*] was 8.21%; thus only about 3½% higher than the average return on fixed-interest loan-values.

Thus, I recapitulate, in the future the German people will have to pay about
12.5 billion [annually] for the various eternal interest-charges of big loan- capital, while the yield from industrial capital in the greatest boom-year was 1 billion, and in times of undisturbed prosperity only 0.6 billion. Thus we see again here a proportion on the orders of magnitude of 20:1 to 12:1.

The third and most dangerous factor is the enormous growth beyond comprehension of big loan-capital through interest and through interest on interest. I must here digress a bit more and hope through a small excursion into higher mathematics to explain the problem. First some examples.

The charming story of the invention of the game of chess is well known. The rich Indian king Shihram granted to the inventor, as thanks for the invention of the royal game, the fulfillment of a wish. The wish of the wise man was that the king should give him one grain of wheat on the first square of the chess-game, two on the second, four on the third, and thus always on each square twice as many as on the one before. The king smiled at the seemingly modest wish of the wise man and ordered that a sack of wheat be brought so that for every square the grains of wheat could be apportioned. As we all know, the fulfillment of this wish was impossible even for the richest prince in the world. All the world's harvests in a thousand years would not suffice to fill the 64 squares of the chessboard.

One more example: many will still remember from their schooldays the torture of calculating compound interest; how the penny invested at the time of the birth of Christ multiplies at compound interest so that it doubles every 15 years. In the year 15 after the birth of Christ the penny has grown into 2 pennies, in the year 30AD to 4 pennies, in the year 45AD to 8 pennies and so on. Very few will remember what value this penny would represent today: a volume of gold equivalent to the volume of the Earth, the Sun, and all the planets combined would not be adequate to represent the value of this penny invested at compound
interest.

A third example: the fortune of the House of Rothschild, the oldest international plutocracy, is valued today
at about 40 billion. It is well known that in Frankfurt around the year 1800, old Mayer Amschel Rothschild, without wealth of his own worth mentioning, laid the foundation for the gigantic fortune of his house through fractional- reserve lending of the millions that Count

Wilhelm I of Hesse had entrusted to him for safekeeping.

Had the accretion of money through interest and interest on interest with Rothschild succeeded only at the modest rate of the penny, the curve would not have climbed so steeply as it has. But assuming that the Rothschilds' collective wealth increased only at the rate of the penny, the Rothschilds' fortune in the year 1935 would be 80 billion, in 1950 160 billion, in 1965 320 billion, and with that it would already exceed by far the total German national wealth.

From these three examples a mathematical law can be derived. The curve that represents the rise of the Rothschild fortune, the curve that can be derived from the number of wheat-grains for the chessboard, and the number that the multiplication of the penny produces at compound interest, are simple mathematical curves. All of these curves have the same character. After initially modest and gradual increase the curve becomes ever steeper and soon practically approaches being almost tangential to infinity.

Altogether differently, however, does the growth-curve of industrial capital proceed. Likewise sprung mostly from small beginnings, soon a strong escalation of the curves appears, until a certain saturation of capital is reached.
Then the curves run flatter, and in certain industries will perhaps even decline slightly, if new inventions have led to the devaluation of existing factories, machines, and

so on. I would like to select only one example here, the development of the Krupp works. In 1826 old man Krupp died almost without assets. In 1855 Alfred Krupp received his first order for 36 cannons

on behalf of the Egyptian government. In 1873 Krupp already employed 12,000 workers. In 1903 Frau Berta Krupp sold the entire works and property to the Alfred Krupp joint-stock company for 160 million. Today the total value of the stock-capital amounts to 250 million.

What does the name Krupp connote for us Germans? The acme of our industrial development. The world's first maker of [steel] cannons. A vast sum of the most tenacious, purposeful, intensive productivity. For hundreds of thousands of our folk-comrades the Krupp endeavor has meant bread and work. For our nation, weapons and defense – and yet it is a dwarf compared to the Rothschild billions. What significance does the growth of the Krupp fortune during a century have compared to the growth of the Rothschild fortune through effortless and endless accretion from interest and interest on interest?

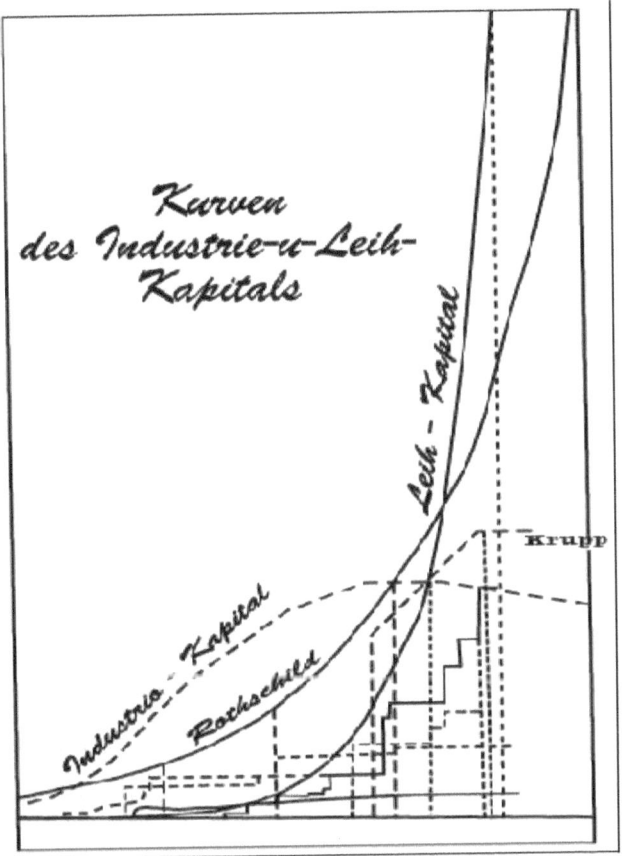

The two curves drawn in bold lines represent loan-interest and indeed the upper curve shows the development of the Rothschild fortune and the lower curve, at first flat and then rapidly rising, shows in a very general way the characteristic development of all such curves, in which a small advance on the horizontal axis can produce a doubling of the value on the vertical axis. The hatched line shows the development-curve of our total industry in the course of the last 40-50 years. The differently hatched fine lines show the development of several randomly selected big industrial enterprises from which the general character of the hatched curve of industrial capital is derived.

It must be expressly remarked that the curves of loan-capital are shown strongly compressed. Thus for example the curve of the Rothschild fortune must be set 80 times so high as the Krupp curve. The purpose of showing the curves of course is only to demonstrate the fundamentally different character of the two types of capital. The curves of loan-capital show at first a quite gradually rising development; the development then goes faster until, ever wilder and dragging everything with it, it raises itself far beyond human concepts and strives toward infinity.

The curve of industrial capital by contrast remains in the finite! However strong the divergences that a trace may show in detail, overall the fundamental character of industrial development will always be such that after strong initial development a certain period of maturity, of saturation, follows, after which sooner or later the decline ensues.

Nothing shows us more clearly the deep essential difference between loan- capital and industrial capital. Nothing can make the difference clearer for us between the devastating effects of loan- capital and the business-profits (dividends) of business-capital put up and risked in large industrial enterprises, than this comparison. It cannot be emphasized enough that the recognition of the mathematical laws that loan-capital and industrial capital follow, alone shows us the clear path
where the lever is to be applied for setting aright our wrecked finance- economy. We recognize clearly that not the capitalistic economic order, not capital in itself and as such, is the scourge of humanity. *The insatiable interest-need of big loan-capital is the curse of all laboring humanity!*

Capital must be! Labor must be! Labor alone can do little. Capital alone can do nothing!

Capital without labor can only be sterile! Therefore the most important demand, the most noble task of the revolution, the most sensible meaning of a world-revolution, is the *abolition of enslavement to interest on money.*

The House of Rothschild today is valued at 40 billion. The billionaires of American high finance, Misters Cahn, Loeb, Schiff, Speyer, Morgan, Vanderbilt, and Astor, are valued together at 60-70 billion at the least. At an interest-rate of only 5% this means an income for these eight families of 5-6 billion, which, according to the researches of Karl Helfferich, is roughly 75% of the annual income that all taxpayers in Prussia had in the year 1912. (There were at that time around 21,000,000 taxpayers, 75% of that would be about 15,000,000. For every taxpayer there are on the average 1.56 relatives; hence 23 million relatives.)

Around 38,000,000 Germans thus have had to live on what the afore-mentioned billionaires have as a yearly income.

Certainly the American billionaires are not pure loan-capitalists in the same sense as the House of Rothschild and so on. I do not care at all to argue about whether the American billionaires are really "100-million-dollar millionaires" or "1000-million-mark billionaires"; in the former case one would just have to reckon in one or two dozen additional Croesuses. Or let us simply accept Rathenau's "300"; then our inventory will certainly be in order. Here it is not important to give an exact number, but the acknowledged ratio of 300 to 38,000,000 opens our eyes about the brutal reign of international loan-capital.

Therefore let us cast off these terrible chains that can only strangle all energetic labor; let us tear away from money the power to bear interest, and ever again to bear interest until all humanity has become entirely obligated for interest to international loan-capital.

Thus it is these three points that make clear to us for the first time where alone the lever may be effectively applied for the alleviation of our internal financial distress.

For another thing, we recognize that the assault of the entire socialist world of ideas against industrial capital has been completely off the mark, because even an intended complete regulation or socialization of all entrepreneurial profit
– assuming an unweakened economy – would yield a laughably meager sum, compared to the enormous financial burdens of the budgets of our Reich and our State.

Through the abolition of enslavement to interest on money the entire financial malaise can be eliminated with one blow. At once we feel solid ground under our feet again; at once it must and will become clear to us that we have only deceived ourselves in the most grotesque manner with this wretched bond-economy.

For what else is loan-capital, but debts? *Loan-capital is debts!* One cannot repeat that often enough. What form of madness is it when the German people in its totality have borrowed 150 billion for its war? When it has even promised itself for this a quantity of 7½ billion in interest and now feels itself shifted into the awkward situation, inevitable from the start, of trying to collect this 7½ billion from itself in the form of entirely fanciful taxes?

* * * * *

The tragic thing about this self-deception meanwhile is less the stupidity of this whole war-bond economy, of which we have always made so much better use than the rest of the world, than the fact that only a relatively small number of big capitalists derives enormous benefit from it, while the entire laboring folk, including the medium-sized and smaller capitalists, as well as business, trade, and industry, must pay the interest. And here the political side of the whole idea comes to light. Here they can recognize that in fact big loan-capital and only this [*i.e.* not industrial capital] is the curse of all laboring humanity. One may twist and turn the thing as one wishes, but always the mass of all hard-working people must in the end bear the cost of interest-payments on loan-capital. The middle- sized and smaller capitalists have nothing to show for their lovely interest-payments; can have nothing to show, for the sums of interest must be entirely taxed away. Whether in the form of direct taxes or indirectly in the way of indirect taxes, stamps, tariffs, or other burdens on commerce, the hard-working folk is always *the sucker* and *big capital* the beneficiary.

It is now quite astonishing to see how the socialist idea-world of Marx and Engels, from the *Communist Manifesto* to the *Erfurt Program* (especially Kautsky), and even the current socialist leaders, spare the interests of loan- capital as if on command. The sanctity of interest is taboo; interest is the holy of holies; no one has yet dared to call it into question. While property, nobility, security of person and possessions, the laws of the Crown, privileges and religious conviction, honor of officers, fatherland, and freedom are more or less outlawed, interest is holy and unassailable. Confiscation of wealth and socialization, thus outright violations of the law that are only somewhat sugarcoated, insofar as they are committed ostensibly in the name of the totality of individuals, are the order of the day: all of that is permitted, but interest, interest is the *noli me tangere*, the "touchmenot."

The interest payment on the Reich's debt is the alpha and omega of the state budget. Its gigantic weight drags the ship of state into the abyss and yet ... it is all a big swindle ... a monstrous self- deception, fostered only and solely for the benefit of the great money-powers.

Here I would like to touch briefly now upon the objections relating to small pensioners, to be discussed later, so that one does not get hung up thinking about them. In the consideration of the very big questions these are not considered, but it goes without saying that these compensations will be provided through the broadest expansion of social-welfare services.

Swindle, I said! *Interest-swindle!* A strong word. But if this word has justification, which during the war was perhaps the most used word in the field and at home, it has the most justification in regard to the interest-swindle.

But what about the war-bonds? With the first 5 billion, the Reich took out of the pockets of the people savings that actually existed. The money flowed back again. Then came the new loan to suck up the money again, and with that the last residual savings. And again came the pump and sucked up the billions, and again they ebbed back again, until merrily, after this charming game was repeated nine times, the Reich had incurred 100 billion in debt.

In exchange the people of course held in their hands 100 billion in finely printed paper – at first we imagined that we had become so much richer – but then comes the state and says, "I am facing bankruptcy."

Yes, but why? – I myself certainly cannot go bankrupt even if I occasionally take a hundred-mark note from the right upper pocket and put it into the left.
Certainly it would be the biggest folly of all if we continued the folly of our war- bond economy by declaring bankruptcy. [* Feder here is regarding the German nation as a unified entity rather than a mere aggregation of individuals: the money that has been

transferred from some Germans to other Germans remains within the German nation, which means that it is within the power of the German government to adjust the distribution, perhaps to the immediate disadvantage of some individuals but for the good of the nation as a whole.]

Let us break the enslavement to interest on money! Let us declare the war-bond certificates to be legal tender with interest canceled, and the nightmare of
state bankruptcy will melt away from us like March snow under the Sun.

People say to me, the cancellation of interest-payments is a disguised state bankruptcy. No, that is not true! – The specter of state bankruptcy is really only a fairytale and a bogeyman invented by the Mammonist forces.

The book by Franz Röhr, *Was jeder vom Staatsbankerott wissen muß* [*What Everyone ought to Know about State Bankruptcy*], is completely stuck in Mammonistic ways of thinking. Although the author in general quite clearly recognizes the economic problems that threaten us through socialization, and although he advises emphatically and correctly that in the end only a rebuilding of our economy can save us – he cannot free himself from the superstitious belief in the sanctity of interest, and therefore he depicts state bankruptcy entirely in accord with the interest of Mammonism, as a completely terrifying catastrophe.

It is interesting to observe that Röhr, in spite of better historical knowledge, cannot free himself from the Mammonistic view, and notes in his closing word: "If the ruinous economic catastrophe is not averted, no one will be spared by it," while on page 81 he admits that the consequences of public financial mismanagement have been partially reversed very quickly, and on page 68 he says that in any case there should be no doubt that Russia (in the last century) overcame these currency- crises without lasting problems. On page 76 he says, while examining the effects of state bankruptcies, that although of course profound economic problems *etc.* have occurred, by and large neither the destruction of the state nor that of its economic strength resulted. *On the contrary a rapid revival of the national economy and a recovery of public finances have been observed often enough.* When the author then continues for three more lines saying that state- bankruptcy absolutely means economic catastrophe and causes infinite misery; I regret being unable to follow this logic.

But back to our particular case! Which would be more honest? To speak pharisaically of the unassailability of war-bonds while oppressing the people with an egregious tax-burden? Or, if a finance-minister had the courage to approach the people openly and to declare, "I cannot make the interest- payments on the war-bonds, or I can only if I collect exactly the same amount in taxes from you. ". . . . But back then during the war I absolutely needed money; nothing more clever (see England) occurred to me, and so I did the swindle with

the high-interest war-bonds. You must forgive me, beloved folk; it was ultimately all for you, but if we wish to play hide-and-seek no more
... I, the state, shall pay no more interest, and you, the taxpayer, need not pay taxes to cover these interest payments.... That thoroughly simplifies our transactions; we avoid the enormous tax-bureaucracy and likewise the enormous interest- paying bureaucracy, thus conserving an immense quantity of money and work- potential."

I have lingered long on exposing this swindle, but I consider it absolutely fundamental here at no point to lose sight of the big picture.

* * * * *

According to Bavarian tax-returns, the circle of people that would suffer -- let us say, precisely those that according to their tax-returns received over 30,000 marks in interest-payments -- are 822 people, which is only 0.4% of those obliged to pay taxes (*Bayr. St-Z.* 1913) in all Germany, therefore, approximately 10,000. (The upper 10,000!)

Let us clarify for ourselves now as briefly as possible the most important aspects of this revolutionary demand, and indeed let us consider the questions first from our national perspective.
For this there is first need of a clear look at our current situation. Secretary of State Eugen Schiffer, in his big speech in the Berlin Chamber of Commerce, has

34

declared it "impossible to ignore." That is only partially correct. *Possible to ignore* is the enormous indebtedness of our national economy, and the unprecedented devaluation of our currency -- in short, the fact that we have become an impoverished people overnight.

The burdens that are being imposed on us through the peace-treaty, however, cannot be ignored. The currently existing certificates of indebtedness, as we have seen, amount to around 250 billion. Let us assume first that the Entente imposes on us an additional 50 billion in war- reparations in some form: that makes a total of around 300 billion in debt.

However heavily it may strain the narrow confines of this treatise, nonetheless some words must be said about the magnitude of German national wealth. The investigations of Helferrich and Steinmann-Bucher assess the German national wealth at around 350 billion. One can only attribute very limited value to such findings, however carefully they may have been derived.
They are valid only for times of undisturbed economic activity. But they are also quite misleading since state and municipal properties are included, thus for example also road-repairs, waterway-modifications, and so on. It is
clear that although the production of such works may have cost enormous money, nonetheless they have strictly speaking no intrinsic value. A better yardstick for national wealth is so-called taxable wealth as it

emerges from the tax-returns for the defense-contribution or the wartime wealth-tax. For this a sum-total of 192 billion results, thus much less by far than Helfferich's figure. To this sum nonetheless about 10% may be added, according to experience, for the legally tax-free small fortunes, and about an equal amount for "silent reserves." [* "Silent reserves" are the result of underestimating positive values and overestimating negative values in accounting, so as to create the appearance of the lowest possible net-worth.]

In any case it seems to me overly optimistic to speak of a national wealth of more than 250 billion. But even this number has only a very limited importance. The most correct thing would be to break away entirely from the idea of a national wealth that is at all numerically graspable, and to penetrate to the recognition that national wealth finds its expression exclusively in the mental and physical work-potential of the entire nation, and thus belongs to orders of magnitude that have no relation to the narrower concept of capital.

Indeed we must still see a further source of national wealth in the presence of mineral resources, the riches of the forest, and fertile soil, but these things also cannot be grasped numerically, since their value fluctuates between zero and infinity, depending on whether the mineral resources lie unexploited, or, based on a geological report, can be reckoned for billions of tons of coal and so on.

Let us not forget that Germany really is a poor country.

Of monopolies it possesses almost none. In wealth of mineral resources it stands far behind most of its neighbors, to say nothing of the unparalleled mineral resources of the Chinese, Indian, and American empires. In fertility of the soil it falls far short compared to the blessed fields of Russia's black soil, and compared to the effortlessly productive stretches of tropical and subtropical land. Therefore in the end we have always only the potential and will of our people to work, as well as the availability of sufficient work, and we must understand clearly that in this state of affairs there can be no talk of secured debts, of collateral for our debt-instruments...

Whether interest-bearing war-bonds or non-interest-bearing Reich banknotes, behind them stands only and solely the tax-potential of the entire people – and what is tax-potential other than a function of the work-power of the total working population?

* * * * *

We must now clarify for ourselves yet another relevant complex of questions, and of course the chief entries of our state revenue-sources and expenditures. There is a remarkable contrast between the broad space that the concern for making money occupies in our private lives, and the attention that we give to the great questions of our state financial management, and yet between individual economy and national economy no essential difference exists whatsoever.

The chief entries for state revenue are: first, the net profits of the post-offices and railroads; second, those of the mines, forestry-administrations, and other state enterprises; third, tolls and indirect taxes; fourth, direct taxes.

So as not to foster purely theoretical discussions in such eminently practical questions, I want to elucidate the individual entries from the Bavarian state budget[1] of the year 1911 according to their order of magnitude. Post, telegraph, and railroads[2] brought 120 million; forests, mines, *etc.*, around 40 million; indirect taxes, 53 million; direct taxes, 60 million. An additional 67 million flowed from stamp-duties, fees, inheritance-taxes, land-taxes, revenue-transfers from the Reich, and so on.

What about expenditures? We find here in the first place the payments for interest on the state debt including the railroad-debts with 85 million. For the royal house, 5 million; administration of justice, 27 million; internal administration, 40 million; churches and schools, 51 million; financial administration, 13 million; expenditures for Reich-related purposes, 50 million; pensions, 36 million. Miscellaneous expenditures 5 million. Back then in this fortunate year of Bavarian finances the annual budget left a revenue-surplus of 27 million.

In the scope of our thought however only those expenditures concern us that can be omitted through the abolition of interest-slavery. Here the interest- payment on the state debt naturally stands in first place at 85 million marks; add to that the greatest part of our payment for financial administration at about 10 million; furthermore a large part of the payments for Reich-related purposes, of which let us add half, 25 million, and finally the 5 million in payments for the royal house are now gone: a total of 125 million.

The disappearance of these entries means the possibility of renouncing imposition of *all direct and indirect taxes*, which, as we saw, brought in 53 million and 60 million marks, a total of 113 million marks!

We are now not at all of the opinion that one should entirely abolish direct and indirect taxes; unquestionably within reasonable limits they serve on the one hand to educate, on the other hand to regulate. It is certainly not more than right and fair that the profits from property owned free and clear remain subject to a moderate, graduated tax, since the state of course must also maintain secure ownership with its policing agencies. It seems just as advisable that trade and industry be required to make tax-contributions corresponding to their working profits, since the state also has to care for the maintenance and development of public paths of commerce for them. A corresponding minimum poll-tax for every citizen entitled to vote is likewise a requirement of fairness, since care for the security of the person and his property is also required from the state.

In the area of indirect taxes a strong expansion of all

pure luxury-taxes has a regulatory effect in the best sense, while all simple foodstuffs and necessities of the people should be kept free of taxes!

The result of such a tax-policy would be found less in high revenues – about which there can be no talk, since for the great mass of the population taxation should be not a real burden but only a reminder that the person is not only an individual essence but also a citizen of the state, and that in addition to civil rights he also has civil duties.

Tax-revenues should be less necessary for paying off the debts of state-owned businesses, whose net-profits, as we have seen, suffice to cover the normal expenditures of the state for schools, universities, administration of justice, internal administration, *etc.* Tax- revenues should be used to advance special cultural tasks of the state for which adequate resources were never available in the scope of the normal state budget. Here I am thinking primarily about orphanages, institutes for the blind and the crippled, daycare centers, care for expectant mothers, the battles against tuberculosis, alcohol, and venereal diseases, and the construction of garden- cities and settlements, especially for the accommodation and humane care of our war-disabled.

* * * * *

Our view broadens. We see virgin land. Could the abolition of interest-slavery mean the cancellation of all taxes? It would mean that, if we had come out of this gigantic struggle as a victorious people. As things are, let us not celebrate too early; the burdens imposed on us by our enemies will make sure that we do not. But in any case we see virgin land based on the indeed quite simple example of our Bavarian state budget that we just used...

In general we find quite similar relationships in the other German federal states, and it is not too much to say that from the surpluses of the state-owned businesses, the railroads, post-offices, telegraphs, forests, mines, and so on, all state expenditures for the entire administration of justice, for all internal administration, including state construction-projects, all outlays for schools and universities, just as for cultural purposes, could be covered without difficulty. Thus a perfectly ideal condition.

Why is that not the case? Interest has crept in. Because of the payment of interest the population's foodstuffs become expensive; because of interest sugar and salt, beer and wine, matchsticks and tobacco and countless other necessities of daily need carry indirect taxes. Because of interest, direct taxes must be raised, which are divided into land-taxes that are passed on in the form of higher prices for grain, house- taxes that drive up rent, business-taxes that burden productive labor, income- taxes that unavoidably depress the living-standards of civil servants and people on fixed salaries, and finally at the very end, modest in giving but insatiable in taking, loan-capital pays taxes on capital dividends. According to the tax-returns of the year 1911, out of 253 million in capital dividends received in Bavaria, all of 8.1 million was paid in state taxes.

We have seen that all capital dividends, all interest on capital, ultimately must be raised through the labor of the entire people. We have seen that the interest- payment on public debts constitutes the largest entry in our state budget, and we have seen that those obliged to pay taxes on interest-payments make only an extremely limited contribution to state revenues.

In terms of relative magnitude, the capitalist paid 8 million out of a total of 60 million in direct taxes, which is only an eighth to a sixth of the direct state taxes paid in Bavaria in 1911. Direct taxes however are only about a fifth of the total state revenue. Therefore loan- capital contributes only about a thirtieth to a forty-eighth share of the state's total needs.

It should not be denied that tax- legislation during the war, especially in the last years, resorted to a stronger tax on capital dividends, but stronger indirect taxation has more or less kept pace with it, so that the relative size has hardly changed.

The picture becomes dire when we consider the budget of the Reich. Here the proportions in themselves are already much less favorable. The Reich does not have the same tax-sources as the individual federal states. Direct taxes are reserved to the federal states; the enterprises of the Reich are limited to the Reich's post-office and railroad (note that this does not include the Prussian state railroads), and consequently only tolls and indirect taxes remain.

The orders of magnitude of the Reich's revenue-sources (see *Statistisches Jahrbuch für das Deutsche Reich* for the years 1917 and 1918) were, in the year 1915, 1 billion in indirect taxes, 0.8 billion in special revenues (war- contribution, matricular fees), and so on. Here too the same picture again. More than a third, 1.3 billion to be specific, was devoured already in the year 1915 by payment of interest on the Reich's debt. Here too loan-capital pushed its way in again. Here too it requires all direct taxes to satisfy it. Sugar pays 163 million, salt 61 million, beer 128 million, tobacco, schnapps, sparkling wine, lamp-fuel, matches, playing cards, and countless other items had to be taxed in order to scrape together a billion marks that then flows completely into the pockets of the capitalists.

Today, how to pay the interest on the Reich's debt is a riddle. Interest- payments alone devour 8 billion [annually], based on 100 billion in war- bonds plus other war-credits. Revenues from the post-office and railroad can hardly be further increased. A further increase in tolls will hardly be tolerated; therefore probably only a five- or ten- fold increase in indirect taxes is left -- an impossibility! -- or the clear insight that only and solely the abolition of enslavement to interest on money can bring us salvation. An enormous self- deception is what the entire war-bond economy was. The German nation borrowed a hundred billion from itself for its war. For that it promised 5 billion in interest to itself; it must therefore pay 5 billion in taxes. All benefit goes to the big capitalist, who draws so much in capital dividends that he cannot possibly use it up, and yet only a quite modest percentage is taken away through the tax on capital dividends, as we have seen.

* * * * *

I hope now through the main thrusts of my presentation already to have dispelled the humanly comprehensible terror that many readers may have of eventually losing the interest-income from their pretty certificates. Let it just be demonstrated very briefly with one example that the whole interest-economy is a big self-deception, and along with that I want to look at an upper level of solid middle-class income.

Assume that the head of a household has an income from labor of 10,000 marks, and on top of that another 5000 marks from capital dividends. In the first place about 1500 marks of this will be paid in direct taxes; then at least 1000-1200 marks in the form of high rents will be stripped away for eternal interest.
Another 1000 marks are likely to be drained off in the form of indirect taxes for a family of five or six, and already now one realizes that not much is left of the lovely capital dividends that the small and middle-sized capitalists enjoyed under the happy tax-rates of earlier years. Indeed, already today there can be no more talk of "surplus"; on the contrary, if one examines for oneself today the current fantastic tax- proposals,

considerably more income from labor will probably be taxed away.

Naturally the situation seems to be quite different for the big capitalist, who, let us say for example, collects only 1 million in capital dividends. (Such people are fairly numerous in Germany today.) Of the tax on capital dividends this fortunate man pays at the most 50-60 thousand marks. Of indirect taxes he also pays no more than the family-father of the previous example. On his budget after all he can still live quite comfortably indeed with 40-50 thousand marks, even in the current expensive era. If roughly a nice 900,000 marks cash remain to him, for that with 5% interest on loans he will get another 45,000 marks in the next year and that, by law, at the expense of the working population.

The small pensioner who only lives on his interest undoubtedly would be harmed. If he is able to work, then he must of course resolve to earn an income from labor. With that he then situates himself very much better than the millions of his folk-comrades who have nothing other than their physical or mental work-potential. If he does not want that, then he must eat into his wealth. Ultimately he has 20 years to nibble at it again and again, if he continues to consume the annual sum that he has been receiving at 5% interest. For persons that are not in a position to work, or are weakened by illness or age, obviously an appropriate livelihood must be arranged through the development of social welfare for all segments of the population.

I visualize social welfare as follows:

Let us assume that an older lady, a widow, who hitherto had to live on the interest from a capital investment of 60,000 marks, is, through the legally proclaimed abolition of interest-slavery, deprived of her source of income. Here, through the broadest expansion of the pension-system, opportunity would be given the afore-mentioned person to draw a pension corresponding to her capital, wherewith the annual pension could even be increased relative to the

previous interest-yield, so as also to give a certain compensation for the diminished value of money even to this circle of people. Thus, for example, in exchange for the surrendered 60,000 marks in debt-instruments of the Reich, of the states, or in covered bonds, an annual lifelong pension of 4000 marks could be given. If the widow has children and she wants to will a portion of the wealth to them, then it can be allowed to her that only 40,000 marks be transformed into a pension, while the remaining 20,000 would be kept for the children. Out of the 40,000 marks, depending on the age of the pension- applicant, up to 1/12 of the received capital could be given annually.

Furthermore, let it also be noted here that, with the discontinuation of oppressive taxes as a result of the abolition of interest-slavery, the widow's cost of living will be quite considerably decreased.

It would greatly exceed the scope of this essay to examine in detail the personal interests of each stratum of the population. Such a revolutionary demand cannot be about personal interests; nevertheless as the idea takes effect one will find that the healthful consequences personally benefit every individual in the end.

Precisely by the problem already isolated above, of how to achieve release from interest on war-bonds, I have tried to make it clear already that small capitalists -- by which I mean all the hundreds of thousands that have been induced through a hyper-American advertising-campaign to devote their savings for subscription to war-bonds -- not only receive no benefit from interest, since of course they must pay for it themselves with taxes, but, with tax- legislation tailored for the protection of big capital, must support interest-payments for million-mark subscriptions.

It seems to me that, apart from these immediate considerations, an appeal to all for the sake of their children's wellbeing must in itself persuade the anxious bondholder to accept as completely natural the renunciation of eternal interest from the Reich's debts. In this case, what does the patriot, who has given 10,000 marks to his fatherland in direst need, really lose, other than a usurious claim to draw 50,000 marks in interest within a hundred years, without even diminishing the principal?
Eternally his children and grandchildren must work, just to pay all the interest.

* * * * *

The question of repayment of the lent sums can be solved in various ways. In my briefly stated main ideas about the problem at hand, which I submitted to the government of the People's State of Bavaria [under Kurt Eisner] on 20 November of last year [1918], I proposed simply to have repayment take the place of interest-payment at the rate of 5% annually for 20 years. I believe that in what follows I can even make a much better suggestion, which because of its simplicity certainly deserves preference: "The war-bond certificates upon cancellation of interest will be declared to be currency." That is the Egg of Columbus. The advantage of this measure is in the first place that nobody really feels anything from it. The war- bond certificates continue to lie at rest in the depots; but no young people get them, any more than a book, or a cabinet, or some otherwise useful object that somebody would lend to his friend.

If one needs money, then one simply whips out a war-bond note and pays with that. War-bond notes have, after all, just as much beauty and paper-value as our other 10, 20, 100, and 1000-mark notes. There can certainly be no talk of the market's being flooded with currency in such a bump-free transition from the interest-economy into the interest-free national economy. All the war-bond certificates are indeed already well protected and stored in bank-vaults, or other places of concealment considered secure by the people, such as a woolen stocking or a manure-heap. Indeed it cannot be denied that our issued paper currency, as much as about 40 billion, is also not in circulation but for the most part is hoarded in the manner described above. Our need for currency in the times of economic boom before the war was also only about 4-6 billion, and it is inconceivable that we would need more than twice that much today in the ever more customary cashless economy.

[In a later section Feder states that he has decided that simply letting war-bond certificates be used as currency is not the best idea. He proposes that they should be converted into bank-credit instead.]

* * * * *

The cancellation of interest is to be done in precisely the same manner for all fixed-interest assets. For these assets, just as for dividend-yielding assets, the originally proposed "repayment" in 20 or 25-year annual pensions is recommended, especially for mortgages.

The abolition of interest-slavery for mortgages means without a doubt the solution of the housing problem, the liberation from exorbitant rents. It is not at all evident why the holder of a mortgage should have the eternal benefit of interest from a sum lent once, why an effortless and endless influx of goods should be granted to him, why the great mass of a people, only for this unhealthy principle of interest, should pay high rents year in, year out. Let it be interjected very briefly that self- evidently there can be no talk of a complete cancellation of rent, since of course the management and upkeep of houses demands constant labor and money. A lowering of rents thus can only occur so far as it results of its own accord through the accomplished repayment of mortgages.

Only one thing should be sharply emphasized, that the abolition of enslavement to interest has not the slightest thing to do with our total value-producing labor, insofar as no hindrance is posed in any way to the entrepreneurial spirit, to productive labor, to the manufacture of goods, to the acquisition of wealth. On the contrary, as we have seen, the entire working folk is liberated from a stifling, unreasonable, heavy burden; our soul- life is purged of an intoxicating poison.

* * * * *

We can tell how correctly the fruitfulness of the interest-problem has been recognized in the course of history, by the fact that minds in all ages and all peoples have been occupied with it...

In various passages of the Old Testament, such as Leviticus 25 and Deuteronomy 15, we find regulations about the cessation of interest in the form that the seventh year should always be an acceptilation or jubilee, in which all debts of folk-comrades should be abated.

Solon in the year 594B.C. abolished personal debt-slavery through legislation. This law was called the great *Seisachtheia* (shaking off of burdens).

In ancient Rome the *Lex Gemicia* of the year 332 B.C. abruptly forbade Roman citizens entirely from charging any interest.

Under Justinian a prohibition on compound interest was enacted, with the regulation that no more interest whatsoever should be demanded when overdue interest has accumulated to the level of the sum originally lent.

Pope Leo I (the Great) decreed in the year 443 a general prohibition on taking interest; until then only clerics had been prohibited from demanding interest on a loan. The ban on interest was now part of Canon Law and also a binding regulation for the laity. Secular legislation also gradually fell in line with canonic views, and even threatened punishment for charging interest. We find this in the police ordinances of the Holy Roman Empire for the years 1500, 1530, and 1577.

Of course such laws were now much opposed and frequently circumvented, and in this quite short historical retrospective it may only be mentioned as an astonishing historical fact that although under the canon law of the 11th to 17th centuries the charging of interest was forbidden to Christians, it was permitted to Jews.

It would be extraordinarily charming to investigate in each instance what economic tumors led to these powerful shedding of burdens. It would be especially valuable to see which powers and forces have violated the prohibitions on interest again and again.

In the Middle Ages certainly short work was often made of usurers; the farmers or citizens having been bled dry got together and beat the profiteers to death. Today we have entered into a completely different phase of the interest-problem. Such pogroms are most deeply disapproved.

Also it is no longer a matter of individual locally confined symptoms of illness that could be combated by excising the pus-pocket; what is happening is a serious sickening of all humanity.

* * *

It should be most emphatically stressed that precisely our contemporary culture, precisely the internationality of economic relations, make the interest- principle so murderous. The foregoing historical retrospective should also not be regarded as providing an analogy for the circumstances of today. When the Babylonians overcame the Assyrians, the Romans the Carthaginians, the Germans the Romans, then there was no continuation of enslavement to interest; there were no international world- powers. The wars were also not financed through borrowing but with treasures accumulated during peace.

David Hume gives a very nice overview of this in his *Essay on Public Credit*.

Only the modern age with its continuity of ownership and its international law allows loan-capital to escalate into infinity. The penny that was invested at interest at the time of the birth of Christ exists no more, because

since then all rights of ownership have had to give way to violence several times; by contrast the penny that old Rothschild invested at interest still exists, and will exist, if there is international law, for all
eternity.

In addition it ought to be considered that broad stretches of the Earth have only in the modern age gone over from natural economy to money-economy. It is quite especially important in this connection that only in the middle of the 19th century were all restrictions on charging interest, and likewise all prohibitions on interest, abolished: thus England in the year 1854, Denmark 1856, Belgium
1865, Austria 1868.

Thus today's concept of interest as inseparable from the possession of money is not much older than half a century. But precisely this interest-concept has for the first time caused money to turn into the demonic power of such universal coercion that we have come to know.

The incipient and then ever-increasing indebtedness of states to capitalists likewise dates only to the middle of the 19th century. Only since that time do we see the state degraded from being the trustee of the folk-community into being the trustee of capitalistic interests. This development has reached its highpoint in war-bonds, which we encounter in all lands, which exclusively, as we have recognized, serve only Mammonistic interests, which should be crowned with the gigantic credit-edifice of a world-loan.

* * *

These brief retrospectives should make it easier for us finally to break away from the supposition that unto loan- capital must be lent the supramundane power to grow eternally and interminably from itself. Gifted with a terrifying potential for sucking dry. We must break away from the notion that loan-capital, unaffected by worldly deeds and misdeeds, should be able to sit enthroned above the clouds, unaffected by transitoriness, unaffected by the forces of destruction, unaffected by the shots of our giant guns. For, should even houses and huts, railroads and bridges shattered by shells sink into dust and ash, the mortgages will still exist; the railroad bonds and public certificates of indebtedness are not thereby erased. Should villages and cities, entire provinces fall victim to the insane destruction of war, what is the result? New certificates of indebtedness are what it means. With eyes flashing greed the Gold International enthroned above the clouds watches the mad rush of humanity. And not long distant is the time when all humanity finally shall serve only as interest-slaves to Mammonism.

The idea is international; it must liberate the entire world. Hail to the nation that first dares the bold step. Soon others will follow.

The question often directed to me, whether the idea is nationally realizable at all, I answer with *yes*. We are internally indebted.

Against foreign interest-claims we are naturally powerless for now; these must simply be paid. Excessive capital- outflow must be blocked to the extent possible, but, as little as the lawgiver refrains from working out laws against murder, manslaughter, fraud, *etc.*, because there would still always be scoundrels, just as little should a people in its totality restrain itself from taking a step recognized as necessary for the healing of its public finances, just because of the fact that not exactly the best elements of the folk are trying to carry their loot into safety outside the country. If we assume that hundreds of millions, even billions in war-bond certificates would be spent abroad; even this could still not be a significant impetus for failing to abolish interest- slavery; for proportionally, of the more than 250 billion marks in fixed-interest domestic investment-assets, by far the majority must still be in the country.

Let us again summarize briefly. – The abolition of enslavement to interest is the radical means for the final and permanent healing of our public finances. – The abolition of the interest- community means the possibility of renouncing oppressive direct and indirect taxes, because the state-owned businesses, especially after the socialization of further suitable sectors (inland navigation, electricity, air- traffic, *etc.*), will give sufficient surpluses to the public coffers to support all social and cultural tasks of the state.

Aside from this financial consideration, the abolition of the interest-community will grant to productive labor in all fields of endeavor the priority that it deserves. Money is returned once again to the role appropriate to it, to be a servant in the powerful drive of our national economy. *It will become again what it is, a voucher for completed labor,* and therewith the path is cleared for a higher goal, for abstention from the raging money-lust of our age.

The idea points toward the establishment of a united front of the entire working population: from the unpropertied laborer who, as we have seen, is very heavily burdened with indirect taxes for the satisfaction of loan-capital, through the entire bourgeois class of civil servants and employees, of the farming and small-trades middle class, which get to feel the pitiless tyranny of money in the form of wretched housing, farmland- rental, bank-interest, and so on, all the way up to the leading heads, inventors, and directors of our big industry, who are one and all more or less stuck together in the claws of big loan-capital, for whom the first task of life is always to work for the sake of pensions, dividends, and interest for the money- powers playing behind the scenes. No less do all circles of the intelligentsia – artists, writers, actors, scholars, as well as other independent professionals – also belong to this group.

Although big loan-capital, as a group of natural persons or as the personification of the interest-principle, seeks consciously or instinctively to conceal the fact of its boundless lust for control, and although our entire legal tradition based upon Roman law, thus upon law serving for the protection of a plutocracy, has ever so strongly emphasized the protection of property and therewith permeated our people's sense of justice, *the abolition of enslavement to interest on money must come, as the only way out of the threatening economic enslavement of the entire world by the Gold International, as one of the ways to drive out the poison of Mammonism with its corruption and contamination of the mentality of our age.*

The Conversion of War-Bonds into Bank- Credit

The demand in § 1, for the conversion of war-bond certificates *etc.* into legal tender, has on numerous occasions been met with the objection that it would mean excessively flooding the market with currency. This objection is in itself quite erroneous. Inflation occurs through the mere existence of war-bond.

It is however true that, in spite of its wrongheadedness, the concern about the physical presence of these papers declared to be currency is not going away, and therefore despite being unrealistic this concern might generate unfortunate side-effects, as if in fact a new inflation had taken place.

Therefore, amending § 1, we demand, after legislative cancellation of the obligation to pay interest, conversion of war-bond certificates, along with other public debenture-bonds, [not into currency but] into bank-credit.

This formulation has the great advantage that the physical existence of war-bonds as paper would cease; the war-bond certificates would be delivered to the Reichsbank by banks, bankers, thrift- institutions, *etc.*, and would be destroyed after a credit-note for the face-value is issued. Therewith nearly every person in Germany would receive a bank-credit, an open bank-account that he could use.

Such a procedure would also have the great advantage that the retention of larger investments in private possession would not be possible, since after the expiration of a specified deadline the undelivered certificates would be declared void.

Furthermore it would at least be possible to control how much war-bond is spent outside the country [thus affecting Germany's trade-balance]. The last point however must not in any way block fulfillment of the abolition of enslavement to interest. Since we really feel too weak compared to foreign countries, we must satisfy (only) the interest-demands that confront us from abroad. Personally I am entirely of the opinion that we should also uphold the cancellation of interest even for foreign bondholders. We need not fear that foreign interest-claims would be enforced by force of arms, since there has been so much progress in returning [from war-madness] to something resembling self-awareness, and never yet in history has a warlike action been undertaken against a great state because of financial measures affecting private persons. It also ought not to be imagined that even the French people would issue an ultimatum to Germany because of the interest-claims of Messrs. Mayer, Schulze, and Cohn from Germany, based on their German war-bonds carried across the border.

Beyond this it would be possible, so as to avoid even the appearance to the rest of the world of a state bankruptcy, to conduct a lottery of the war-bond, which then of course could easily be rigged based on statistics obtained through the required delivery of certificates, so that at first just the numbers presumably belonging to people abroad would be drawn and paid off in Reich banknotes.

Yet a third thing would be the welcome ascertainment of the distribution of war-bonds, and the accompanying opportunity that still exists for an extraordinarily simple collection of the wealth-tax, while the bursaries of course would need only to instruct the Reichsbank offices to charge the account of Mr. N.N. with so and so many marks in tax. In this manner tax-payments would be more painless by far -- although of course the taxpayers' right of appeal would continue to exist in its full extent.

With such a transformation (conversion) of war-bonds into bank-credits a certain social leveling could also be accomplished, insofar as smaller investments in war-bonds, thus all small subscriptions of all of those for whom the subscription of war-bonds really is to be accounted a patriotic deed; let us say up to 5 or 10 thousand marks, would be made good at par, while all larger subscriptions could be credited at a rate to be established. The credits for all other government paper would be handled precisely the same.

Special Comments on the Demand for Law in the Manifesto

On § 1

It is completely indispensable that all state and municipal debt-subscriptions be treated in the same way, since only such a unitary large-scale regulation of our entire monetary system, hand in hand with the abolition of interest-slavery, can be implemented.

On § 2

It is already clear that the abolition of interest-slavery must be applied simultaneously to all the other fixed-interest papers, so as not to cause an absurd boom in these papers, which obviously would occur if the public papers alone were declared interest-free. The reduction of the debt as such would be accomplished through annual repayment, whereby a constant and consistent un-debting of all debt-laden objects would be accomplished.

On § 3

This paragraph is very closely related to the preceding ones, as well as with the demand for nationalization of mortgage- lending in § 5. The farmer or homeowner burdened with mortgages continues, after as before, to pay the amount that he had to pay to his creditors, but no longer as eternal interest, rather as repayment.

Thus after 20, 25, or 30 years, depending on the preexisting interest- rate, ownership of land and home will be freed from debt. (The mortgage-bank for its part can naturally likewise only during this time continue correspondingly to pay interest on covered bonds to covered-bond- holders.) Hand in hand with this liberation from debt arises the community's right of ownership in the real-estate freed from mortgages.

A universal registry of dwellings, or rather a real-estate cadaster, would have to come first; because debt-free real- estate ownership naturally also has the right to repayment of invested capital, and also a permanent claim on a portion of the rent, to pay all the charges, expenses, and so on that come with real- estate-ownership, as well as appropriate compensation for work that the owner himself does. [* The connection between the registry of dwellings and the rights of debt-free owners is puzzling, unless the idea is to manage the growth of rental property so as to keep it reasonably profitable.]

Let us consider this in broad outlines with the example of an urban apartment- house. The house has a value of 100,000 marks. Against that is recorded a mortgage-bank's investment of 50,000 marks at 4% in position 1, a noncorporate investment of 20,000 marks at 5% in position 2, and 30,000 marks is the amount put up by the house-owner himself. The revenues from rent are 7000 marks. From this must be paid 2000 marks for the first mortgage, 1000 marks for the second mortgage, and 1000 marks for expenses, outlays, and so on: in all 4000 marks. Thus 3000 marks remain to the house-proprietor as an interest-payment [so to speak] for his own invested capital of 30,000 marks.

Following implementation of the legal abolition of interest on money the situation after ten years is as follows: 1st mortgage 30,000 marks, 2nd mortgage 10,000 marks. The house-owner has completely recovered his capital-investment, but on the other hand there is a new, public right of ownership in the amount of 50,000 marks. With that the right of the state to have a say about further income from rent and to determine the amount of rent begins. [* Feder does not state how he derives the figure of 50,000 marks: it is half the value of the apartment-house, but also equal to the amount of the corporate mortgage. Probably the most important fact is that it is not more than the amount owed in mortgages, and therefore causes no pain to the house-owner. Presumably, given the emphasis that Feder puts on painless transition, if the amount owed on the house were less than half the value, the state according Feder's plan would still not claim a share of ownership greater than what is owed on mortgages.]

It would be unjust now, in regard to repayment, to put

the house-proprietor on the same level as mortgages. For his capital is not pure loan-capital in the narrower sense that should be affected by the abolition of interest-slavery; here we are talking about "risk" capital, specifically about money converted into a valuable good, specifically a house. It is therefore up to the owner of the house whether to grant a longer duration of payments, or a corresponding percentage permanently included in the operating expenses of the house.

It cannot be the purpose here to make any binding proposals; here only suggestions are being made as to how a frictionless transition of the interest- economy into the interest-free economy could occur even in the area of real- estate.

So as to complete the example, let the status after 25 years be presumed as follows: by that time all mortgages are paid off; only the permanent expenses are the same or, because of the greater age of the house, increased from 1000 marks to perhaps 1500 marks. Let the return afforded to the house-proprietor from this sum also be about 1000 to 1500 marks; thus accordingly it appears that around 3000 marks of the rent- revenues go to cover non-negotiable charges, while the remaining 4000 of the original 7000 in rent-revenues would be freely disposable. The state thus has the possibility of lowering the rents by more than half; it will do this *e.g.* in workers' dwellings, or the state may cut rents by only 20, 30, or 40%, and thus gain from the difference an enormous source of revenue for other public necessities, above all naturally for publicly conducted home-construction. For mansions the rents are not lowered, or not lowered much, whence very great additional means become available also for the better construction of homes, or for special social purposes. This future state of affairs however reveals – and I hold this for a very fruitful prospect – the inner justification for the community (state) even now to take part in determining the amount of rent in the manner that I sketched above, with a lowering of rent for workers' dwellings.

In the growing right of the state to participate in real-estate-ownership also lies the foundation for a sound bank of issue, and issue of credit to mortgage-creditors.

On § 4 and 5

These paragraphs demand the socialization of the entire monetary system. Money is only and exclusively a voucher for completed labor issued by a community that has its own state. To issue money-tokens is one of the sovereign fundamental rights of the state. The counterfeiting of the state's money-tokens is subject to the most severe punishments; thus *it is a quite forceful social demand that the monetary system be placed under the control of the collectivity.* The work-power of the collectivity is the sole substrate of money-tokens, and only the failure to appreciate this fundamental fact has led in general to the deterioration of our public finances and to complete anarchy of the monetary system in general.

With the surrender of personal and commercial credit by private bankers, proposed in § 5, a deeper incision is made into the total credit-system. For the state credit-system, as well as for municipal and even real-estate credit, one must cleave to the abolition of interest-slavery with utmost rigor and energy, because it is the indispensable prerequisite for the social state in general.

The situation is different with personal credit. We also demand, in and for itself, the interestlessness of personal credit; yet this demand does not carry the same enormous and principal importance. We remember the 250 billion in fixed- interest loan-capital compared to the only 12 billion in dividend-paying stocks.

All such credits, stocks, participation- certificates, mining shares, equity- holdings, and so on, are risk capital. The yield of this capital depends on the industry and efficiency of those persons to whom the money was entrusted. Here the element of risk and danger of loss thus comes into play, along with the question of personal trust. For that, a certain compensation of a special kind still appears indispensable. The owner of stocks and so on is in no way compensated or benefited if the enterprise to which he entrusted his money earns nothing. He loses his money entirely if the enterprise collapses.

It is otherwise with, for example, the owner of debenture-bonds of the *Reicheisenbahn*. The Reich's railroads [in Elsaß-Lothringen] are completely lost with the loss of Elsaß-Lothringen. Nonetheless the holder of railroad- bonds continues to receive his interest- payments. From whom? From the taxes of the collectivity. The railroads may work with a deficit balance of any magnitude as in Prussia and Bavaria in the last year; yet the bondholders receive their interest-payments just the same.

From whom?
From tribute paid out of the work-potential and consumption of the working population.

One would just like to make this fundamental distinction perfectly clear, in order finally to recognize where it is that the vampire sucks from the work- potential of the people.

Thus personal credit should remain, or rather be allocated again, to personal dealing through the private bank. The personal efficiency of the credit-seeker, with which the banker is personally familiar, should again become the determining factor for personal credit. The fees set by the state will regulate themselves by themselves, in accord with the fluidity of money that will in any case commence with the abolition of interest-slavery.

On § 6

The main point of § 5 is also valid for dividend-assets in particular. In the interest of the social state-community it must be demanded that a repayment of the capital once lent be attempted also for the great industrial enterprises – in order to bring about here too a reduction of the indebtedness of the individual industrial works toward those that are only investors.

For in fact what we were able to observe in the relationship of loan- capital toward all peoples repeats itself here on a smaller scale. Here too the capitalist exploits the worker, the foreman, the engineer, the entrepreneur, all equally, because the compulsion to have to earn dividends takes priority. [* This is a problem of joint-stock companies. Companies owned free and clear by families, as is common in Germany, do not have this characteristic.]

If however we attain the liberation of industries and businesses from the eternal interest-sucker, then the way is clear for the lowering of prices of products, and for the delivery and distribution of surplus value, partly to the community, partly to the laborers, middle management, and boards of directors of the particular enterprises, thus to those that really alone create manufacturing and values.

On § 7

In this paragraph naturally the entire field of insurance also comes into play, which can be constructed on an analogous interest-free basis. The premiums paid cannot grow through addition of interest; rather the insurance- companies will become thrift- institutions; in other words the risk and advantage of insurance are retained. For this the political community has to be responsible.

On § 8

With regard to the devaluation of our money, which has resulted only through the enormous mass of our innumerable certificates of indebtedness, we demand a strongly graduated wealth-tax. We lay the emphasis in this on "strongly graduated."

A [flat] wealth-tax [for the purpose of] reduction of the number of notes and so forth would be nothing but a self- deception whereby one throws sand into the eyes of the people. For if I also confiscate half of all of the wealth everywhere and receive payment in bonds and pulp these, all that is really accomplished thereby is a diminution of the amount of paper, while in return a conversion-factor will increase the fictive value of the totality of circulating paper to the same level as before. Real value belongs always only to goods for consumption and goods for use, never to the paper vouchers for completed labor.

Another question is whether the foreign exchange-rate of our mark-currency can be improved. But even this improvement of the exchange-rate is again in the final analysis only dependent on work- potential and production, in other words the possibility for production of our total national economy.

The Objections and their Refutation

Never yet has an idea been able to establish itself without opposition, least of all an idea that makes such a radical departure from the long-established assumptions about the sanctity and inviolability of interest. With the objections already raised and those expected there is always a two-fold observation to be made: it must be asked, first, what part of the objections being made is based on deliberate distortion of the idea of abolition of interest-slavery, and second, what ought to be said in response to all sincere and fact-based misgivings?

The most frequent objection is the assertion: without the charging of interest nobody will lend money

We do not in fact want anyone to lend his money anymore. Credit was the trick, was the trap, into which our economy entered, and in which it is now helplessly ensnared.

If the folk really urgently needs greater capital, then it gets the needed moneys interest-free at the central state treasury, with only repayment required.
Eventually it will issue new banknotes. Why should it issue interest-bearing certificates?! Whether the paper bears interest or not makes no difference! It's only and sole backing is the work- potential and tax-potential of the folk. Why burden every public expenditure from the beginning with the leaden weight of eternal

interest?

Yes, but how should the state fulfill its cultural labors for the community? It still needs money and can be fair in this task only by way of loans that charge interest.

This assertion is based on an entirely Mammonistic way of thinking. It would have to be deliberately calculated for misdirection after thorough reading of this *Manifesto*; for in the first place we have proven that after the abolition of interest-slavery all cultural and social tasks of the state can be covered out of state-owned businesses, out of the revenues of the postal service, railroad, mines, forests, and so on, without anything further. In the second place the sovereign people's state [*Volksstaat*] has the power, at any time, to take care of special cultural tasks through the issue of interest-free value-tokens in lieu of the interest-bearing certificates declared to be the rule in the Mammonistic state.

It is thoroughly impossible to see why the state should make special cultural tasks, *e.g.* railroad, canal, and hydroelectric construction, more costly for itself with an eternal promise of interest that is completely unnecessary. If it cannot pay the costs of construction from the revenues of its current state-owned businesses, then there is no reason to see why the state should not create the money; the sovereign people must indeed pay for it, while it recognizes precisely this money as a means of payment. Why however should the folk, with its entire work- and tax- potential, stand behind another slip of paper (the interest-bearing loan), which imposes on the folk in its totality only an eternal interest-obligation for the benefit of the capitalist!? Therefore away with this obsession of the Mammonistic state!

The capitalists then will just take up the issued paper notes and accumulate paper money.

This is refuted in two ways. First, the demand that mere possession of money should be rendered unprofitable would then of course be already fulfilled, and the abolition of interest-slavery voluntarily undertaken by the capitalists themselves, since the capitalist renounces interest of his own accord if he piles up his paper notes at home.
Second, the capitalist's fear for his money makes it unlikely; one need only imagine the sleepless nights of the currency-hoarder who keeps great sums of money piled up at home and must constantly see his possession threatened by thieves, robbers, burglars, house-searches, fire, and flood. I am convinced that the upright citizen would become tired of these worries in a short time, and would soon find his way to the state bank. The state bank issues a receipt and is now legally responsible for the account, but not for any interest-payments. Otherwise of course a third possibility still remains open to everyone, specifically to work with his money, to create values and to manufacture goods, to participate in industrial undertakings, to render his life ever richer and finer, to support art and scholarship, in short to make beneficial use of his money while

rejecting the Cult of Mammon.

It can however still happen that private need of capital for some goals urgently presents itself, e.g. for testing of inventions, founding of businesses by young, competent craftsmen or businessmen, etc.

To begin with, this has nothing whatsoever to do with the abolition of interest-slavery! For, in the first place, one must logically assume that the capitalist, who after the abolition of interest-slavery of course has no more opportunity to invest his moneys in a bombproof manner and to expect idle consumption of interest, will rather, as in an earlier age, be inclined to risk his money for such purposes, so that a lack or need in this direction will therefore occur much less than hitherto. Or has one not heard on the contrary again and again from the efficient businesspeople, from the cleverest inventors, precisely the complaint of how difficult it is to get money in the Mammonistic state for such purposes unless a "dividend" could be guaranteed? In the second place, it must be the task of the coming state to foster every competent force through generous support. There were indeed even before now already beginnings toward this in the old bureaucratic state, but so small- hearted that, instead of a stimulus, an inhibition and reluctance resulted, because of the harassing regulations that accompanied the granting of public support. In the third place let it be noted that with the allocation of several million marks, enormously much could be achieved. The joy of labor, the industriousness and tenacity of the

German inventor, engineer, craftsman, *etc.* is so great that, through the state's right of participation in the results of fortunate inventions, the expenditures most likely would be richly rewarded (England as an example).

The abolition of interest-slavery leads necessarily to the exhaustion of wealth.

Oho! Who claims that? But of course! Whoever has adapted his life to the consumption of his interest-payments on capital and cannot resolve to work, with him it is certainly true: consuming 5% annually he will have completely exhausted his wealth in 20 years. Of course, but that is indeed completely in order! What we want is precisely the abolition of interest-slavery; we want living on a pension to cease being the citizen's highest ideal. We want to end this Mammonistic decadence; indeed we want no longer to tolerate that one, that many, can live in comfort permanently
only from interest-payments on loans -- in other words at the expense of others!

I repeat: it is also not true at all that the abolition of the lordship of interest would lead to the elimination and exhaustion of wealth. On the contrary, the abolition of interest-slavery would promote the creation of wealth based on labor that manufactures goods and produces value, unburdened and liberated from eternal interest-outlays.
The abolition of interest-slavery leads, as we have seen, to a comprehensive lowering of costs in all of

life; it unburdens us from the excessive weight of taxation so that for every working man the possibility of accumulating savings must be greater in the future than hitherto. One more thing! The goods- and values-producing national-economic labor of industry, commerce, and trade is in no way hindered, but fostered to the utmost through the abolition of interest-slavery.

What does the worker get if capitalists receive no more interest-payments?

This question really ought not to be coming up anymore! In the first place, of course it was the constant battlecry of labor that the capitalists would exploit the workers; in the second place we have indeed clearly and plainly seen that it is the laborer more than anyone else that is required to pay the interest on loans. [In other words, what the worker gets is lower taxes and a lower cost of living.]

The bonds of family are weakened and damaged if one can leave no wealth behind for the children.

Yes what is the reality here? Quite generally I think that money has little or nothing to do with the sense of family. Or has one heard that the children of wealthier parents cleave to their parents more than those of poor parents? Or do rich parents love their children more than the less propertied? What is likely to be more important for the children, that their parents arrange for them the best possible upbringing and have them learn some discipline, raising them into industrious and healthy and courageous people, or that they leave behind for them the biggest possible moneybag?

In particular cases a justified striving to secure the children's financial future undoubtedly will have to be acknowledged. This striving, and thus the thriftiness of the parents for their children, will be in no way adversely affected by the abolition of interest- slavery; on the contrary. The possibility of saving will become greater, when our national economy will be liberated from the all-encompassing pressure of interest-slavery.

We have seen from the example of the man with earnings of 10,000 marks and pension-income of 5000 marks that all medium-sized and smaller fortunes are in fact robbed of any beneficial effect by the circuitous route of the direct and indirect taxes of housing-rent and so on. I cannot repeat often enough: interest on bonds for possessors of small and medium amounts of wealth is a swindle, a self-deception, a running around in circles, but big capital through its devoted press has quite diabolically propagated and proclaimed in all the world the faith in the sanctity and inviolability of interest. It allows everyone seemingly to take part in the lovely, anaesthetizing consumption of interest, in order to lull to sleep the bad conscience that must invariably accompany idle, laborless consumption of interest – and in order to recruit comrades for the struggle, for the defense of this highest good of Mammonism.

The civil servant, the statesman, will say: the state cannot renounce the obligation that it has undertaken toward its creditors.

What does "obligations" mean? Is it in any way moral to enter into obligations about which the state must know from the beginning that it can only fulfill these obligations if it takes the interest away from the creditors through direct and indirect taxes in precisely the same amount? Where is the morality in that?

Or is it not perhaps more honest to admit: "I can only pay the interest if I collect just as much in taxes – but back during the war I absolutely had to have money, and for that I did the swindle with the war-bond; you have to forgive me, beloved folk; it was ultimately for you, and now we want to play no more hide-and-seek; I the state am paying no interest and you, the taxpayer, need not

pay taxes for the interest; that will substantially simplify our transactions. Thus we shall do without the enormous tax-bureaucracy and likewise the extraordinary interest-serving bureaucracy. Right? Do we have a deal?" And you, Herr Scheidemann, do not again post your name on every advertising pillar as the secretary of state of the old compromised government amid foolish declarations relating to the security and inviolability of the war-bond. You only embarrass yourself: the benefit of the entire swindle has indeed gone only and solely to big loan-capital.

Financial officials and banking professionals are

declaring that the abolition of enslavement to interest on war-bonds and public debts is impossible because it is synonymous with public bankruptcy.

You will forgive me: according to your speeches we are indeed publicly bankrupt anyway, or must become so. An overt declaration of public bankruptcy however would be the greatest stupidity that we could commit: to the actual incompetence of the current power-holders it would add prematurely the historical confirmation of this incompetence.

Why declare bankruptcy? If I have put 3 marks from the right pants-pocket into the left, I must still not on that account declare the bankruptcy of the right pants-pocket!

It was indeed no different with the war-loan! The Reich took out of the people's pockets the first actually present billions, then the moneys flowed back again; then came the new loan and again the money streamed back; once again came the pump and sucked the billions and again they ebbed back, until, after the game had been repeated nine times, the state had merrily generated 100 billion in debt. For that the people had 100 billion in finely printed paper in their hands. At first the folk imagined that it had become so much richer; then came the state and said: "It is horrible; I have 100 billion in debt and face bankruptcy." – Yes but why? That is in any case only a self-deception! I myself can indeed never become bankrupt if every so often I take my money from the one pocket and place it in the other.

Therefore we can rest at ease about state bankruptcy in regard to our internal war- bond debts. Therefore we really need not declare public bankruptcy and we can really spare ourselves the gigantic labor with the stupid interest-payments and the big, but even stupider, taxes.

Let us indeed finally free ourselves from doing the bidding of big loan-capital! Only big loan-capital benefits from this loan-interest tax-swindle, since a lovelier lump of gold is left over for it and the laboring folk pays this surplus in the form of indirect taxes; meanwhile, however, the small and middle-sized capitalist simply chases his own tail.

The global economic official says: The abolition of interest-slavery is not possible for us to accomplish in Germany alone; it must be done internationally; otherwise we shall lose all credit, capital will flow away, and we will still have to fulfill our interest-obligations toward the rest of the world.

I confess that I myself was at a loss about this question for the longest time. It is the most difficult question because it involves our relationship with the rest of the world; meanwhile the matter has two sides. On the one hand, the idea of the abolition of interest-slavery is the battlecry of all productive peoples, against international enslavement to interest on money; on the other hand it is the radical cure for our internal financial woe. But it is really no reason to refrain from using a cure, just because the equally sick neighbor does not employ it at the same time. It would however be added stupidity if we in Germany continued to run in a crazy circle and pay taxes and interest when we have clearly recognized that this ridiculous activity benefits only the big capitalists and nobody else. Therefore let us lead the way by our liberating example; let us liberate ourselves from the enslavement to interest on money, and we shall soon see that the force of this victorious liberating idea will stimulate the peoples of the world to follow us.

I am actually convinced that our initiative – if this initiative is not suppressed by the German Mammonists will sweep the other peoples along with irresistible necessity.

The Spartacist says: The whole idea only amounts to a protection of capital; it still remains then as it was: the poor man has nothing and the rich remain.

Yes, my friend; it is in general very hard to have a discussion with you -- if you really are in the depths of your soul a Communist, and will therefore actually maintain that "all things belongs to all men" [* Peter

Kropotkin, *The Conquest of Bread*], and if along with that you are indeed familiar with the actual ideas of the great Bolshevik leaders in Russia, especially Lenin, and regard them as correct, and accordingly regard the next tasks of the Soviet Republic designated by Lenin, "universal tendering of accounts and control of all production and distribution," as humanly possible.

If however you are completely clear about the fact that this task is really only feasible, if at all, under a horrible tyranny, and you still remain at the bottom of your heart a convinced Communist or Spartacist and so on, then let us not dispute further with each other; we just do not understand each other and are speaking different languages, and the future will decide, either for the strait-jacket state that can ultimately result from the chaos of Bolshevism, or the new state for which I hope, with a national economy liberated from interest-slavery.

But if, at the bottom of your Communist heart-- if you are honest -- you find that you still think about, still long for wife and child, for a human soul that stands closer to you than an Eskimo or a Zulu kaffir, if during factory-labor commanded by the soviet-director you think that it would still be nice to possess your own little cottage, a little garden-plot, if indeed in the very depth of your soul it would really give no true satisfaction that you should be entitled like a dog on the street to use every bitch that crosses your path, if you want to call somebody your wife, if you merely think about saving something from your wage, which then should belong to you alone, then you are already no longer a Communist; then you have already in your heart broken from your so loudly proclaimed catchphrase, "All things belong to all men"; then precisely what you do not want is that all things should belong to all men; you want that precisely what you wish for yourself -- wife, child, house, farm, savings -- whether you already have it or only hope to get it, even then should *belong to you alone.*

And do you see, my friend, if you only suspect in your heart that it might make a difference to you, if some random individual came and simply took your savings away from you in the name of "all," and if he brought another child for you and took with him yours because all children belonged to "all," then my friend, let us not continue to speak completely past each other.

Perhaps I could ask you to contemplate whether in fact the Communist message that all things should belong to all men would not necessarily mean *the end of every culture*, because the lack of any concept of ownership must with compelling logic force man down to the level of the beast.

If all things belong to all men, if a tendering of accounts and control of all above-ground production and distribution in Lenin's sense could be coerced, then in the best-case scenario an ant-colony would result. But in that case we can also do without language, soul, and thought; mutely and instinctively we can perform our forced labor. *The end of man is there.* [* "The End of Man" is from *Ezekiel*. There it means the purpose of man but here it could have a double meaning. Man's purpose under Communism becomes mindless slavery, which is the destruction of man.]

But enough now, friend Spartacus. Let this fundamental consideration sink deeply into your head and heart. A more exact answer to your question will then result during conversation with the other parties.

And now, you comrades of the two socialist orientations, moderate and independent! [* Feder refers here to the Social-Democratic Party and its pacifist offshoot, the Independent Social- Democratic Party.]

I cannot imagine that serious contradiction or objections against the abolition of interest-slavery would come from your side, and yet I must deal with you categorically, along with the entire socialist world of ideas, from Marx up to the current leaders Ebert, Scheidemann, Kautsky, and so forth.

> 1. The socialist will: *elevation of the working class* is an idea unconditionally bound to prevail; *so far we are in agreement.*
> 2. The paths trodden for the attainment of this great goal are almost entirely wrong, because they
> 3. are based on false assumptions.
> 4. The [Marxist] socialist idea of the state leads necessarily to Communism, thus to decline.

> 5. Because however Social- Democracy has a different goal, the elevation of the working class,

of all working people in general, it faces a terrible inner conflict, because the logical consequences of Marxism lead to the direct opposite of the practical goal of the workers' movement.
6. From this inner division results the overt uncertainty in the direction of the government.

7. For the sake of the great practical goal (elevation of the working class) a sharper line must be drawn against Spartacus and Bolshevistic Communism, and their methods must be combated with all our might.

8. But Social-Democracy, organized through labor-unions, feels weak today before these radical groups, because it has taken up Marxism thinking as it's fundamental principle of education, and because all Marxist ways of thinking lead to Communism.

Now the proof: point 2 says that the paths trodden by Social-Democracy are almost entirely wrong.

The whole agitation conducted throughout the country has led to a deep division within the population of our nation. The constantly repeated slanders against employers of every kind, indeed of every bourgeois calling whatsoever, as exploiters and bloodsuckers of the manual laborer working ostensibly unassisted, have led to an unjustified embitterment and to the haughtiness of labor, which today necessarily finds its expression in the demand for the "dictatorship of the proletariat"

(*Communist Manifesto*). The essential demand of the *Erfurt Program* – the transfer of the means of production from private ownership into the ownership and operation of the community – has today been compressed into the cry for "socialization."

It is completely clear to every serious politician that

full socialization of our economic ruin would mean complete state bankruptcy. But one dare not confess this openly and freely to the people.

Not *socialization* but *desocialization* would have to be the motto now. Thus one attempts to compensate the blatant miscarriage of every socialization through delusional tax-projects and by this route to "expropriate the expropriators" for the second time. All of that means nothing other than abandoning the entire national economy to utter ruin. Instead of growth (a doubling of production, as the entire socialist literature for the period after the revolution promised, is out of the question) the exact opposite has occurred.

The worst thing however would be if the current socialist government thought of accepting big foreign loans. With that not only would our economic decline be sealed, but we would furthermore quite entirely deliver ourselves into interest-slavery to the Entente, from which there would be no return.

The fundamental failure, the basic error, upon which this whole wrong chain of treaties, demands, and promises to the people has been constructed, is an entirely wrong attitude toward industrial capital and

loan-capital. The *Communist Manifesto*, the *Erfurt Program*, Marx, Engels, Lasalle, Kautsky, have not recognized the *radical difference* between industrial capital and loan- capital.

On this point the entire Social-Democracy must relearn; this fundamental error must be clearly recognized and frankly admitted without reservation. Then however one must also relentlessly draw the only possible conclusions. These however signify radical renunciation of the pointless, because completely mistaken, rage against industry, against the employer. *Worker and work-giver belong together;* they have the same goal —work, production; for without productions, without work, there can be no life, no culture, no forward and no upward. The self-evident and unavoidable oppositions that exist among humans, just because they are humans, just because they are humans, are much less important than the great shared interest of employer and employee. These oppositions are and have been resolvable by means of wage contracts and trade organizations to the mutual satisfaction of both sides.

But let us not pursue further these questions that are trivial in the scope of our treatise on the largest political lines of force, and let us only emphasize that the interest of labor collectively is perfectly aligned with our national industry, with the national economy of our people.

Whoever teaches otherwise and presents the oppositions between employer and employees as more important reveals himself as irresponsible precisely in regard to the workers; for he thereby lays the axe to the roots of the tree that nourishes and supports the worker.

Social-Democracy however *has* done that, and with that it has incurred eternal guilt before German labor; with that it has brought unspeakable misery upon our folk, *because it cannot keep all its promises, because it cannot bring to us the peace of mutual understanding, because it cannot create work for us, because it must even set up an armed force against us, because it cannot get by without the civil service, because it must demand the obligation to work, because universal equal and direct suffrage for men and women over the age of 20 helps nobody to earn a living, because without the state's guarantee of the security of person and property chaotic circumstances must occur, because without integration and subordination of the individual into society no vitality of the state is possible.*

Thus a deep, despair-filled wave of disappointment passes through the entire people. If individuals still do not understand it, ministers, members of parliament, and people's delegates continue cheerfully lying to each other that the "gains of the revolution" must be defended against "reaction": what these two terms mean, if anything, no sincere statesman would be able to tell the people clearly.

The negative actions of the revolution, the *deposing* of a series of antiquated dynasties, *deposing* of officers, *abolition* of the nobility, *dissolution* of the

army, in short the "Great Demolition," is indeed no

"gain."

And reaction?! The swept-away, rotten doctrine of divine right does not have anywhere in the entire folk enough moral support to result in any forceful action; the bourgeoisie, as regards the real *bourgeois*, is much too cowardly, much too morally corrupt, to rally against class-conscious labor: therefore it is not necessary for the ruling class of the workers to be worried about a dynastic or bourgeois reaction.

But the deep disappointment of the people about the so-called gains of the revolution, in other words about the lack of any real improvement of the people's situation, that is the great danger. This disappointment leads to the streaming away of great masses ever farther to the left, where the promises already made are outbid by far.

Ultimately one can no longer make promises such as "all things to all men." That is pure madness, but every idea, every phenomenon, every activity stretched and exaggerated to the extreme becomes madness in the end, and then changes into its opposite. So goes it likewise with the Communist idea that all should belong to all, for this ultimately comes to an end and resolves into all ... having nothing. Hunger, despair, misery, sickness, and need have arrived in Russia; people have lost the last remnant of courage and joy in living.

I repeat: the enormous fundamental error in the socialist idea-world is ultimately to be traced back to the failure to recognize the deep essential difference between industrial capital and loan- capital. *Interest-devouring loan-capital is the scourge of humanity.* It is the eternal effortless and endless growth of big loan-capital, not productive, goods- manufacturing, industrial working-capital, that leads to the exploitation of peoples.

I cannot forgo here the examination of the question of *why* this essential difference has not been recognized; whether it really has not been recognized, or whether it perhaps has been obscured for the benefit of big loan-capital; whether the leaders and chiefs in the struggle against Capitalism, whether the authors of the *Communist Manifesto*, of the *Erfurt Program*, and the current leaders always have proceeded with the necessary conscientiousness.

It is the most grave and terrible thing when one casts doubt on the absolute earnestness and firm conviction of another; it seems all the more grave, the more carefully one seeks after the causes and relationships pertaining to life's occurrences. I want therefore also to give no answer at all to this question itself, rather only to allude to big, obscure connections by citing an utterance of Disraeli, the greatest English Prime Minister, Lord Beaconsfield. This he writes in his novel *Endymion:*

> "No man will treat with indifference the principle of race. It is the key of history, and why history is often so confused is that it has been written by men who were ignorant of this principle and all the knowledge it involves." [Baron Sergius to Endymion]

The bourgeois.

The bourgeois, to whom rest appears as his bourgeois duty, is certainly disturbed by every new revolutionary demand, as always with every new idea. It means unrest for him; for perhaps he would even have to think something about it.

All change is odious to him; he wants to have his rest, and woe unto him that covets his moneybag. Now indeed one does want from him his interest- payments, his income from rent on houses, the interest-payments from his covered bonds, the interest that he collects on mortgages; in short, what constitutes his rest, his contentment, and his good fortune.

Even so, we must inquire what the members of the classes owning loan- capital will have to say. They form, apart from the true bourgeois....

Bourgeois is a human type, with which nothing further is to be initiated; the bourgeois is a branch on the tree of humanity that should be lopped off, the sooner the better. These are the smug, self-satisfied Babbitts with their deplorably narrow horizons, who are capable of no enthusiasm. They while away their days in eternal monotony with coffee, morning newspaper, morning drink, noon paper, lunch, afternoon nap, coupon-clipping, afternoon drink, friends at the pub, and occasionally the movie-house. Lacking comprehension for all that moves the world, all for which youth longs, all that distresses the folk, the state, and society, untroubled about war and victory, they vegetate and decay, simultaneously arrogant and obsequious – but the bourgeoisie is such a broad class that it cannot be ignored.

Thus, through the abolition of interest-slavery, thrift is destroyed; people end up in the poorhouse.

That the abolition of interest-slavery quite generally may have its influence on thrift must be decisively denied. Thrift has just as little to do with the prevailing economic views as *e.g.* wastefulness. Thrift and wastefulness are human qualities that either are present or not, indifferent to whether an age approves or frowns upon the idea of interest.

In times of transition perhaps an increase or diminution of thrift can be promoted. In the given case however I tend much more to the view that a rational, economically minded person will say to himself the following: "I can no longer in the future count on living on my interest alone. I want however to live in later years and also still leave something behind for my children; therefore I must now save more." The abolition of interest-slavery must, in my opinion,

exert this effect on the majority of people. As for the elderly, of course they will be referred to public support.

Here too I must once again stress emphatically that, given the current burden of direct taxes on property and the burden of indirect taxes on every lifestyle, nothing of the lovely interest-payments remains, except in the case of that person for whom – and it is indeed something iniquitous and to be combated

– all income flows *only* from eternal interest-payments. Therefore a decline in thrift is probably not to be feared.

Is (loathsome) big capital really so utterly unfruitful? Has it not also created the means to large-scale progress that bears fruits for humanity greater than what the interest on loan- capital destroys?

No! The posing of the question only proves that Mammonistic phraseology has clouded our clear vision.

Big capital has not created the means to large-scale progress; rather big capital has grown from labor! All capital *is* accumulated labor. Big capital is in itself unproductive, because plain money by itself is a thoroughly unfruitful thing. From mind, labor, and available or already developed raw materials or mineral resources, values are produced and goods are manufactured – through labor and only through labor.

For if one pours so much money onto the most fertile farmland, into the richest coalmine, the farmland does not on that account bear grain, nor the coalmine spit out coals by itself! Let us conclusively affirm this.

If people have invented money, it is accordingly quite useful and reasonable; for in every complex economy one needs this (universally recognized) "voucher for completed labor." But that a potential should inhere in these "money- empires" to grow eternally from themselves into enormity – and money does that, if it can bear interest – it is that against which the core of our being rebels; it is that which exalts money far above all other earthly manifestations; it is that which makes money into an idol. And all of that is indeed only the most enormous self-deception of humanity!

Nothing, nothing at all, can come from money alone.

Table, cabinet, clothing, house, tool, in short everything around us has some value; in the end one can still use a broken piece of furniture as firewood to warm oneself, but with a twenty-mark note one cannot do anything; I cannot even wrap a piece of cheese in it. Only after people have sensibly agreed on the facilitation of the exchange of goods for consumption, to write vouchers for completed labor, only with that does the slip of paper receive meaning and purpose, and it is very reasonable that the farmer for his grain receives from the coalmining company not coal but money; thus a voucher for other completed labor, *e.g.* pitchforks, crockery, plough, and scythe. But with that the power of money should end.

Thus the large-scale progress of humanity has been made not by money but by the men themselves, their bold spirit, their proud daring, their clever mind, the strength of their hands, their *shared*, therefore *social*, industrious labor. So proudly and so clearly must we see. The men were the thing, certainly not the pitiful pieces of paper that men invented for the simplification of commerce.

Further Program

Although the abolition of interest- slavery is not the final goal of the new statecraft; it is truly the most incisive deed, the only deed that is able to unite all peoples into a true league of nations, against the tyranny of Mammonism that encompasses all peoples. But it is not the end. On the contrary, the abolition of interest-slavery must lead to further steps, because, as we have seen, it lays hold of the global evil by the root, and indeed by the main root.

Only when the ground laying demand for abolition of interest-slavery is fulfilled, is the path cleared for the first time ever for the social state. This must be clearly recognized, and it must be accomplished in spite of all Mammonistic powers. The cry for socialization [while interest-slavery persists] is nothing more than the attempt to bring about the formation of a trust of all industries and to create giant conglomerates everywhere, over which big loan-capital, in spite of all wealth- taxes, will naturally also have the deciding influence again in the future. A socialistic state on a Mammonistic foundation is an absurdity and leads by nature to a compromise between Social- Democracy, already strongly contaminated with Mammonism, and big capital.

We, by contrast, demand radical rejection of the Mammonistic state and a reconstruction of the state according to the true spirit of socialism, in which the ruling basic idea is the obligation to nourish -- in which an old basic demand of Communism can find its rational and useful satisfaction -- in the form that *every* member of the folk shall receive his assigned entitlement to the soil of the homeland through the state's allocation of the most important foodstuffs.

We further demand, as a skeleton for the new state, a representation of the people through the Chamber of People's Representatives, which is to be elected on the broadest basis, and next to that a permanent Chamber of Labor, the central council in which the nation's workers have a voice in proportion to their distribution by profession and economic class. Finally we demand the highest accountability for the directors of the state. This new construction of the state on a socialist-aristocratic basis will be treated in an additional work that will appear soon from the same publisher.

The prerequisite for all this construction however remains the abolition of interest-slavery.

My unshakable belief, nay more, my knowledge makes me recognize clearly that the abolition of interest-slavery is not only enforceable but will and must be taken up everywhere with indescribable jubilation. For bear in mind: in contrast to all other ideas and movements and endeavors, however well intentioned, that aim at the improvement of mankind, my proposal does not want to try to improve human nature; rather it applies itself against a toxic substance, against a phenomenon that was artfully – no, diabolically – invented, completely contrary to the deepest feeling of man, in order to make humanity ill, in order to ensnare humanity in materialism, in order to rob from it the best thing that it has, the soul. Hand in hand next to it goes the frightful, pitiless tyranny of the money-powers, for which people are only interest-slaves, exist only to work for the dividend, for interest.

Deeply troubled we recognize the frightful clarity and truth of the old Biblical proverbs, according to which

the god of the Jews Yahweh promises to his chosen people: "I want to grant to you to own all treasures of the world; at your feet shall lie all peoples of the Earth and you shall rule over them."

This global question is now laid out before all of you. Global questions are not solved with a wave of the hand, but the idea is clear as day. And the deed must be diligently propagated; we must understand clearly that we face the most formidable enemy, the world-encompassing money-powers. All force on the other side, on our side only justice, the eternal justice of productive labor.

Extend your hands to me, working people of all countries, unite!

www.ingramcontent.com/pod-product-compliance
Lightning Source LLC
Chambersburg PA
CBHW021134300426
44113CB00006B/423